NEW ROAD!

by Gail Gibbons

HarperCollins*Publishers*

NEW ROAD!
Copyright © 1983 by Gail Gibbons
Printed in Mexico   All rights reserved.
10 9 8 7 6 5 4 3 2

Library of Congress Cataloging in
  Publication Data
Gibbons, Gail.
  New road!

  Summary: Describes the planning and
construction of a new road.
   1. Roads—Design—Juvenile literature.
2. Road construction—Juvenile literature.
[1. Road construction]   I. Title.
TE149.G5 1983   625.7   82-45917
ISBN 0-690-04342-2
ISBN 0-690-04343-0 (lib. bdg.)

Special thanks to Arthur Hill, Jr., and
Arthur Hill, Sr., of Hill-Martin Corpora-
tion; Kevin Hayes of Pike Industries;
LeRoy Carlson and Donald C. Brown of
the State of Vermont Agency of Trans-
portation; Sergeant Ernest Strong of
the Vermont State Police.

To start, the road planners are called in. A group arrives to study the traffic on the road. They count the number of cars and trucks going by.

A roadblock is set up for trucks. The trucks pull over
to weigh in at the weigh station.

Now the planners know how much traffic and how heavy
a load the new road will have to carry.

On a nearby site, other planners come to study the land.
Surveyors measure the distances between ground points.
Sample takers drill to find the layers of rock and
collect soil to study.

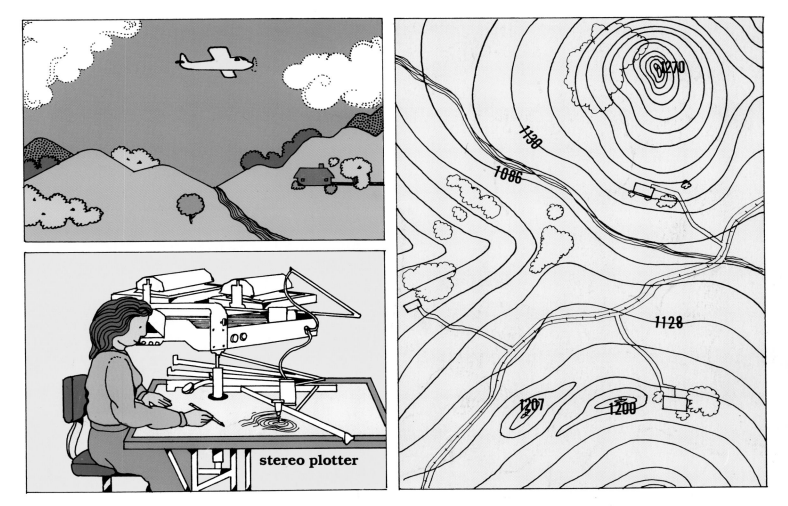

A surveyor plane flies over the site taking photographs. From these, a contour map is made showing the high and low points of the land.

Now all the collected information is fed into a computer. The computer will help find the easiest, safest, and least expensive way to build the new road.

The planners study feedback from the computer. Then they plan the exact route the road will follow, how wide it will be, and the type of construction materials to use.

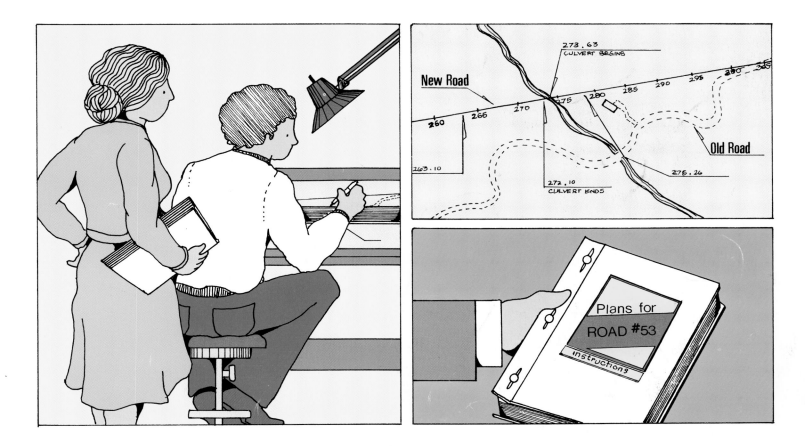

The plans are given to draftsmen, who draw the route in detail. Another team works out all the instructions for the making of the road.

The road will go across some private land, and now the land must be bought from its owner.

The drawings and instructions are taken to the site.
A second survey crew takes measurements and sets out
stakes marking the center of the new road.

A contractor is hired to take charge of the road's construction. He studies the drawings and instructions with his work crew.

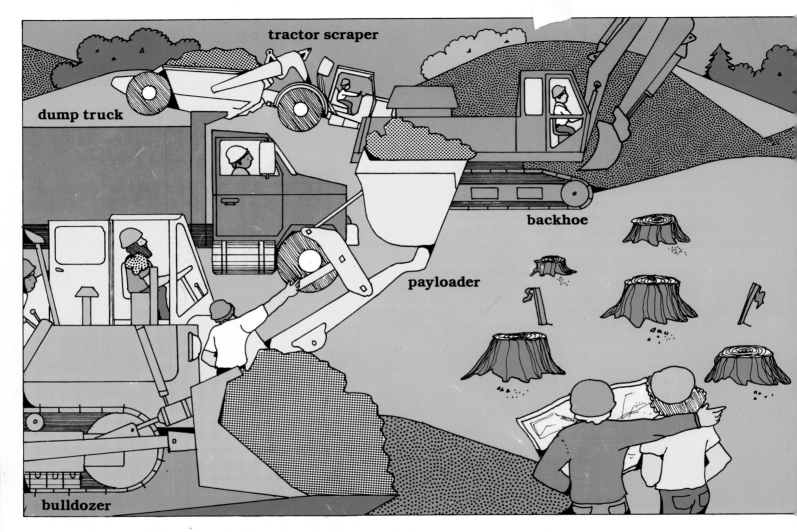

The work begins. Big machines come to clear the way for the road.

logging truck

Trees are cut down and hauled away.

power grapple

bulldozer

A round, metal culvert is placed in the ground where there is a stream. The water will flow through the culvert underneath the roadbed.

payloader

bench-drill crawler

dump truck

Whole ledges of rock are blasted apart.

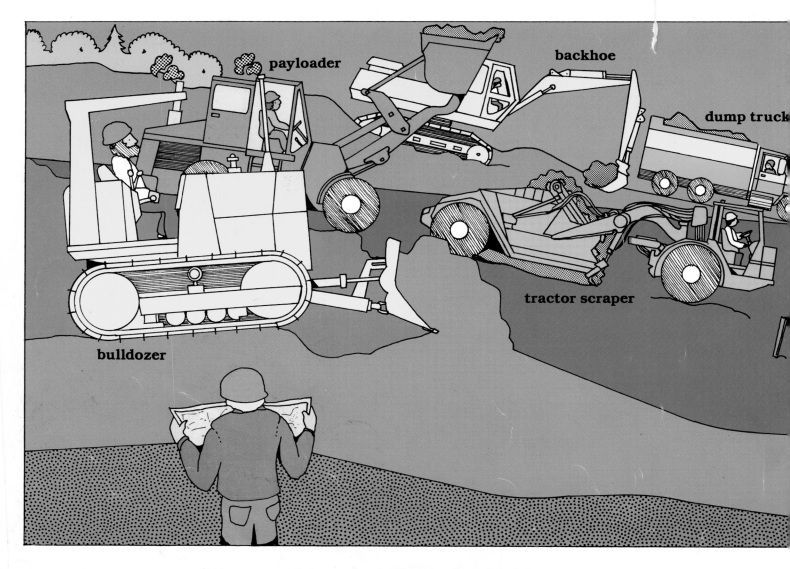

Other machines cut through hillsides...

using the dirt and rock to fill in lower places.

The dirt is pushed back and forth to make a level, smooth roadbed. Then a compactor packs it down.

Truckloads of rock are delivered to the roadside.
The rocks are put through a crushing machine to make
small stones. The stones are spread onto the roadbed
and a compactor packs them down to make a firm base.

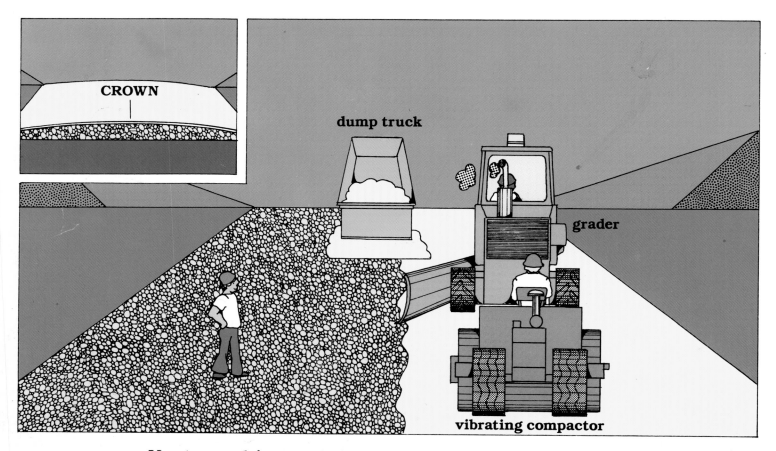

CROWN

dump truck

grader

vibrating compactor

Next, sand is poured on the stone base. A vibrating compactor shakes the sand down into the gaps and packs it in tight.

The center of the road is made higher, so when rain falls it will run off to the sides.

asphalt

asphalt paving machine

This will be an asphalt road. An asphalt paving machine moves onto the roadbed. Dump trucks line up and take turns pouring their loads into the front of the paver.

As the paving machine inches forward, a layer of hot asphalt spreads out behind it.

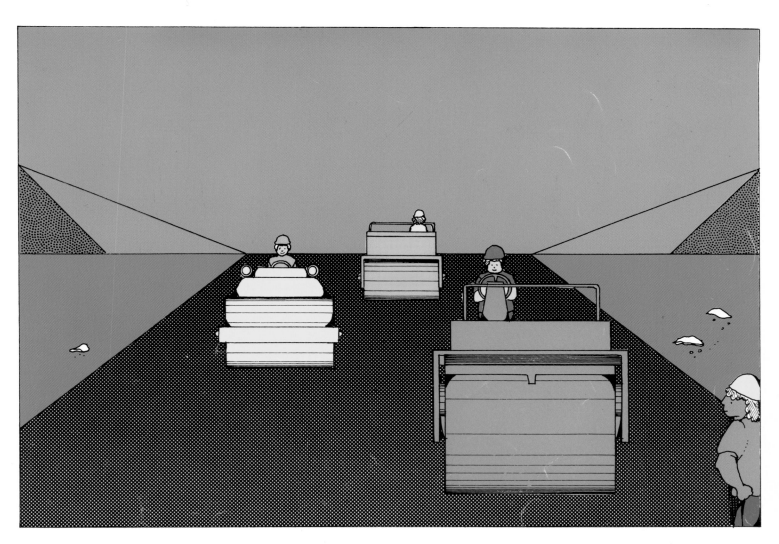

The asphalt is packed down, and it cools into a hard, rough surface.

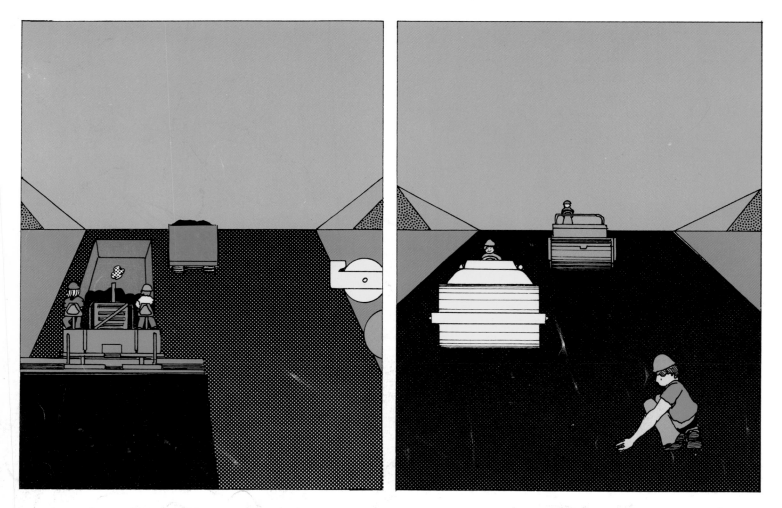

Again the paver spreads a layer of asphalt onto the road.
Compactors pack it down, and this time it cools into a
hard, smooth surface.

A roadline painter truck paints lines to mark the lanes.

cherry picker truck

road
service
truck

SPEED
LIMIT
55

A road crew places signs along the roadside.

Lights are set in place.

Trees, bushes, and grass are planted to make a pleasant view
for drivers and to keep the soil from washing onto the road.

The road is finished, and it is beautiful.

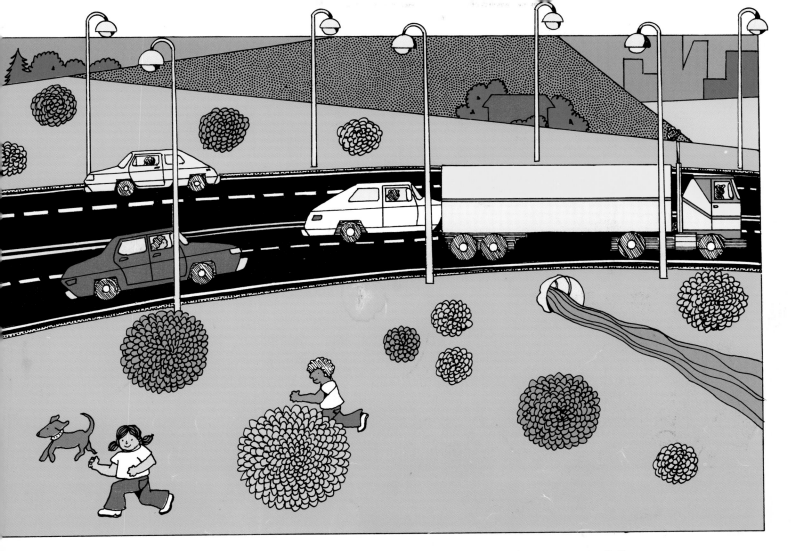

The cars and trucks move faster and more safely now.
The new road will be used for many years to come.

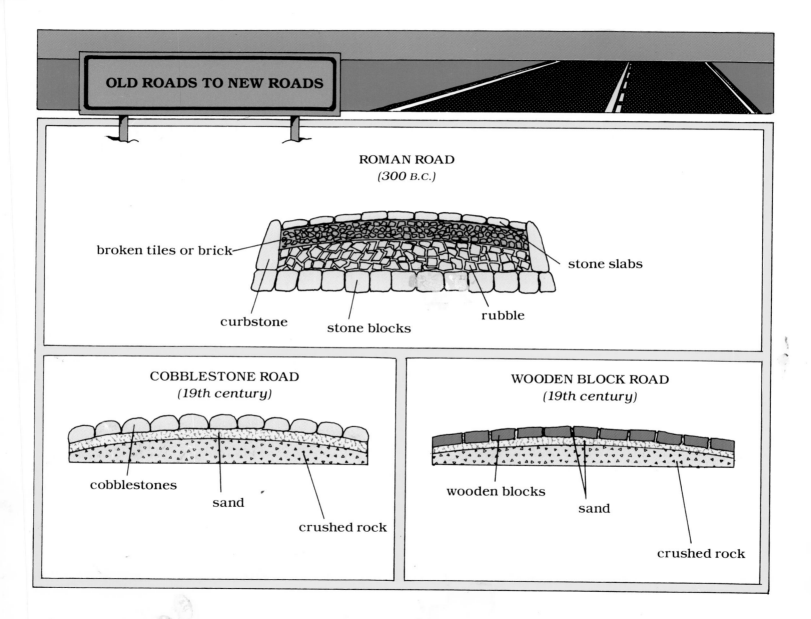

OLD ROADS TO NEW ROADS

ROMAN ROAD
(300 B.C.)

broken tiles or brick

stone slabs

curbstone

stone blocks

rubble

COBBLESTONE ROAD
(19th century)

cobblestones

sand

crushed rock

WOODEN BLOCK ROAD
(19th century)

wooden blocks

sand

crushed rock

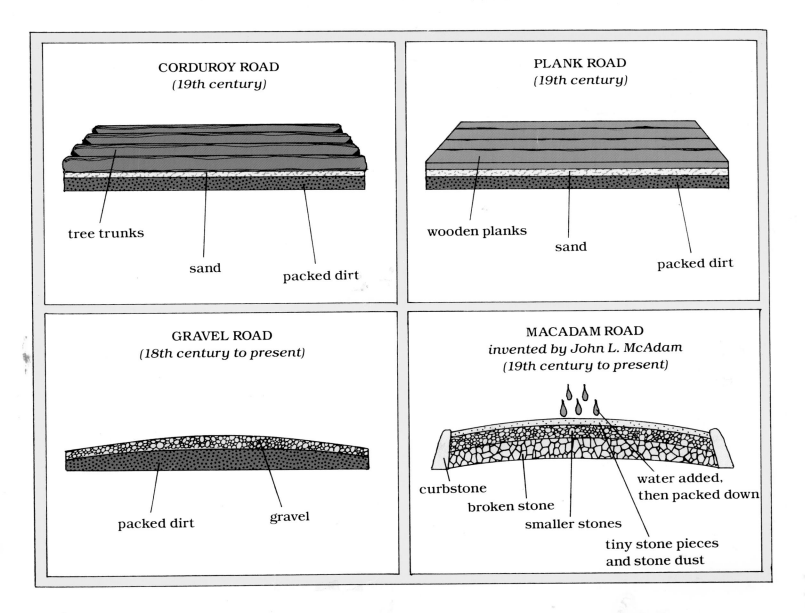

CORDUROY ROAD
(19th century)

tree trunks

sand

packed dirt

PLANK ROAD
(19th century)

wooden planks

sand

packed dirt

GRAVEL ROAD
(18th century to present)

packed dirt

gravel

MACADAM ROAD
invented by John L. McAdam
(19th century to present)

curbstone

broken stone

smaller stones

water added,
then packed down

tiny stone pieces
and stone dust

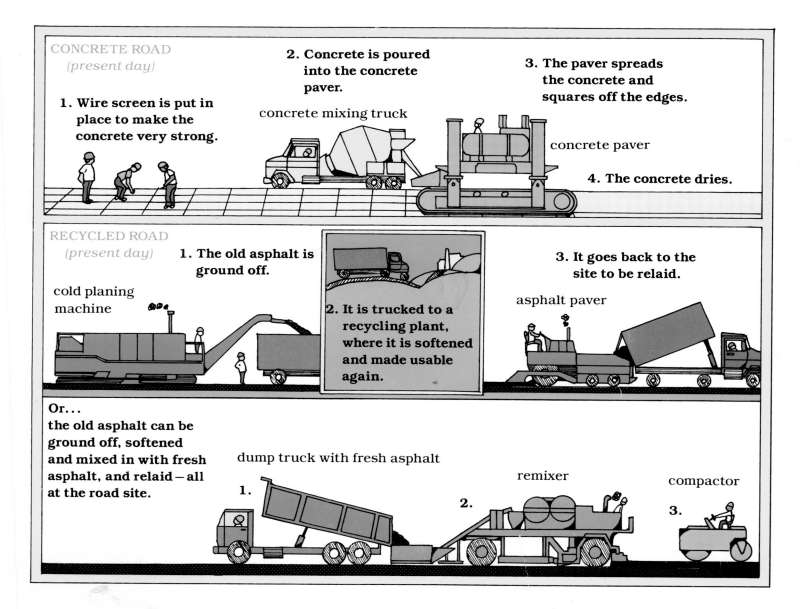

CONCRETE ROAD
(present day)

1. Wire screen is put in place to make the concrete very strong.

2. Concrete is poured into the concrete paver.

concrete mixing truck

3. The paver spreads the concrete and squares off the edges.

concrete paver

4. The concrete dries.

RECYCLED ROAD
(present day)

cold planing machine

1. The old asphalt is ground off.

2. It is trucked to a recycling plant, where it is softened and made usable again.

3. It goes back to the site to be relaid.

asphalt paver

Or...
the old asphalt can be ground off, softened and mixed in with fresh asphalt, and relaid — all at the road site.

dump truck with fresh asphalt

1.

2.

remixer

compactor

3.